FRANCES POET

Frances Poet is a Glasgow-based playwright and dramaturg.
Stage plays include *Gut* (Writers' Guild Best Play Award winner,
UK Theatre Best Play Award nominated and Bruntwood Prize
For Playwriting shortlisted; Traverse Theatre and Tron Theatre,
2018 and in a French translation as *Madra*, Théâtre La Licorne,
Montréal, 2019), and the multi-award-winning *Adam* (Scottish
and UK tours, 2017/18, and NYU Skirball Centre, 2019).

Frances has also completed a number of classic adaptations
including *The Macbeths* (Citizens Theatre/Scottish tour, 2017/18),
What Put the Blood (Abbey Theatre, Dublin, 2017, and
previously as *Andromaque* Scottish tour, 2015), *Dance of Death*
(Citizens Theatre, 2016) and *The Misanthrope* (Oran Mòr, 2014).

Frances's play *Crusaders* is part of NT Connections 2020.

Work for screen includes the Glasgow drama series *River City*,
and work for radio includes *Gut* (Radio 4), and *Alt Delete*
(Radio 3).

Other Titles in this Series

Frances Poet

FIBRES

NICK HERN BOOKS
London
www.nickhernbooks.co.uk

A Nick Hern Book

Fibres first published as a paperback original in Great Britain in 2019 by Nick Hern Books Limited, The Glasshouse, 49a Goldhawk Road, London W12 8QP, in association with the Citizens Theatre and Stellar Quines

Fibres copyright © 2019 Frances Poet

Frances Poet has asserted her right to be identified as the author of this work

Cover design by Amber Keating

Designed and typeset by Nick Hern Books, London
Printed in the UK by Mimeo Ltd, Huntingdon, Cambridgeshire PE29 6XX

A CIP catalogue record for this book is available from the British Library

ISBN 978 1 84842 846 1

Woodland
CARBON
www.woodlandcarbon.co.uk
NICK HERN BOOKS
Printed on Carbon Captured paper

A Stellar Quines and Citizens Theatre co-production, *Fibres* was first performed on 17 October 2019 at Barrowfield Community Centre. The cast was as follows:

BEANIE	Maureen Carr
PETE	Ali Craig
LUCY	Suzanne Magowan
JACK	Jonathan Watson

Director	Jemima Levick
Set and Costume Designer	Jen McGinley
Lighting Designer	Emma Jones
Sound Designer	Patricia Panther
Assistant Director	Louise Shephard

Acknowledgements

Thank you to Fiona and all the team at Playwrights Studio Scotland for the New Writing Award, without which this play might not exist, to Chris Hannan who mentored me with a gentle excellence and rigour, and beautiful Cove Park, where I wrote the first draft while Oma and Grandpa took care of the kids.

For their input and support thanks to Morven McElroy, Ron Donachie, Ryan Fletcher, Barbara Rafferty, Ashley Smith, Jen McGinley, Gary McNair, Andrew Rosthorn and Benjamin Hannavy Cousen.

My family (Richard, Peter, Elizabeth and Mimi) – I couldn't do it without you. Giving thanks too for my granddad, Richard Rosthorn, who 'plight his troth' to the wonderful Annie Whitaker and embarked on a sixty-year long happy marriage.

Thanks to the lovely Nick Hern and eagle-eyed Sarah Liisa Wilkinson.

Huge thanks to the team who have worked to get the play on stage: the brilliant staff of the Citz and Stella Quines, Dominic Hill who championed the play, shaped and improved it, the exceptionally talented Maureen Carr, Ali Craig, Suzanne Magowan and Jonathan Watson and my dear friend, Jemima Levick, who has brought the play to life with such skill and sensitivity – thanks, pal.

All of this starts with Eli Poland, who told me about her beloved mum and dad who she lost too soon. I never met them but they have fuelled the love, pain and anger carried in this play. Remembering them now...

Elizabeth and Ian Higgins Macleod.

F.P

For Richard.

This one's for you, baby.

Characters

BEANIE, *sixties*
JACK, *sixties*
LUCY, *thirties*
PETE, *thirties*

This text went to press before the end of rehearsals and so may differ slightly from the play as performed.

Snow

A mountain of clothes, crumpled and neglected.

In front of it stand LUCY *and* PETE *and* BEANIE *and* JACK *all facing the audience. Snow is falling on them.*

LUCY. It's snowing! And he says it like he's a seven-year-old or something. Wide-eyed looking up at the sky. Total joy. And then he looks at me. And it's like somebody has pressed mute on the sweaty party in our office above. And I don't know this guy. Not really. And he doesn't know me. But we're breathing together as the snow falls like little angel kisses on our faces.

Both of us totally switched on. And I lean into him. He touches his hand to my face and it feels... like goosebumps and I know –

BEANIE. He's going to propose.

LUCY. He's going to kiss me. And then I'll be his.

BEANIE. I know he's going to propose because we've agreed we'll get married. He's got the okay from my da and everything so... I just don't know when. And we're walking home from the pictures, hand in hand and it starts snowing and I think. Now. Now would be nice. And I slow down a little because he'll have me back to my ma's door before we know it and the moment will have passed. So I'm dawdling. And he's rabbiting on about the car Steve McQueen was driving in the picture and the snow's melting on my hair and dripping down the neck of my dress and I'm thinking, it's passing, the moment is passing. Come on, Jack.

LUCY. Mum and Dad got engaged in the snow...

BEANIE. Come on. Come on.

JACK. It's like being in a cunting snow globe.

LUCY. I don't know why I do it. I stroke my hand along the wall. And I shove a fistful of snow in his face.

JACK. 'Snowball!'

PETE. It always snows at Christmas.

LUCY. He looks so shocked. Expecting a wee kiss and now the ice is dripping off his face. He looks like he might actually cry and... I'm off. Pegging it away from the black-and-white-movie perfection.

PETE. In films anyway. Doesn't it? Christmas and snow go together like... well, two things that go together. Like buckets and spades, haggis and neeps, humanity and the crippling knowledge that we all die alone. If the air is full of anything at Christmas, it's supposed to be snow.

BEANIE. I've stopped walking completely by now and finally he clocks it and falls silent. I nod at him and the penny drops and he fumbles about in his pocket for a while to get out the ring his mother's given him for me. He gets down on one knee and says, 'Beanie, I plight thee my troth,' which was an odd way of putting it but I got what he meant. I said yes and we had a little kiss and then he walked me home. Not quite like the movies, but it was... nice.

LUCY. I run and I run until I'm miles away from the kiss that could have been and the colleague I've fancied for the best part of three years. I'm cold and wet and I'm a fucking idiot. And I need to be with people who can help me understand why I'm like this, why I run when I should stay and all of a sudden I'm at a door, letting myself into the warm safe cocoon of my childhood home like I'm a teenager again. But one step in, I know my parents are rowing. Neither of them says a word but Mum is letting off a round of tutting like machine-gun fire as she irons my dad's underpants, while he lobs a retaliatory grenade of silence her way.

And it's colder in here than it is outside and I understand everything more clearly than I ever hoped to. And all I want to do is to quietly let myself out again and step back into the snow.

JACK. A couple of the men are lobbing snowballs at us. One lands on this fella who's working, and he's none too pleased.

He brushes it off his overalls, all 'stop pissing about' and 'what are you, a pair a kids?' And they're shouting at him to lighten up. They lob one at me. I catch it and chuck it back, clocks one of them right in the face. Wipes the smile off him for sure.

But it's a laugh. Group of men mucking about together and I think, this is better than school this. This is gonna be okay. My wages in my pocket after a hard day's graft. This is alright.

Sun's blazing outside and in here we're having a snowball fight. White stuff everywhere, falling like snow.

The snow stops being beautiful and becomes oppressive. There's too much of it and it's getting in LUCY*'s mouth and eyes. The mood has changed.*

LUCY. This isn't snow?

JACK. Just looks like snow. Not the real thing.

LUCY. It's not even wet.

JACK. It's the dry stuff you've to watch out for.

LUCY. What is this?

PETE. Expecting snow, ash is what I got.

JACK. You breathe it in and it takes hold of you.

LUCY. What the fuck is this?

PETE. Seven years old waiting for Christmas and everything is falling down around me except for snow.

JACK. Kills you from the inside.

LUCY. Get it off me!

BEANIE. Look at the state of you.

BEANIE *takes* JACK*'s coat from him.*

LUCY. No...

BEANIE *is shaking the dust off* JACK*'s jacket.*

Don't do that, Mum. Don't breathe it in!

Introducing Beanie

BEANIE (*putting on a pair of latex medical gloves*). It's the
gloves. I'm not squeamish about the dressings or the yellow
fluid draining from Jack's chest. I manage the clamps fine.
I even quite like watching the vacuum in the bottle start to
draw the fluid down the tube. Like squeezing a really ripe
spot. It's the latex gloves. I can't bear the touch of them.
Pulling them on to my hands, tight around every finger. Feels
like I'm putting on a… [condom] well, you know. I never
liked touching those either. I know why you have to use
them. The gloves. We haven't worried about the other things
for years. Risk of infection – I've read up on it. Got to wear
the right equipment for any job. Jack's helped us both learn
that the hard way. I wear the damn gloves and throw them
off soon as I can. But this morning the phone rings soon as
I've finished putting the clamps on. So I'm still wearing the
gloves when Dr Sleeman tells me they've got the results of
my chest X-ray and could I make an appointment to come in
and see her…

And I know then that it's got me too.

*She pulls off the gloves, disgusted by them, and throws them
to the floor.*

Introducing Lucy

LUCY. 'What's the difference between a woman and a washing
machine? The washing machine doesn't ask you for a cuddle
after you dump a load in it.'

Overheard one of the technicians tell that one. Doesn't make
any sense. It assumes blokes actually do their own washing.
They don't. The women do. Every relationship without fail.
I lived with a couple at uni and we all washed our own stuff.
They get together, a few years pass, they have kids – now
she washes clothes for five people, says her life is one long
cycle of moving clothes from one place to another. I've

never heard of a single relationship where the guy does the washing. Not one.

Not having to wash somebody else's shit is the best thing about not being in a relationship.

What's the difference between a woman and a washing machine? There is no fucking difference.

Introducing Pete

PETE. I'm having a really shitty day.

Long pause. Eventually he realises everybody is waiting for him to say something.

Oh, no that's it. That's all I wanted to say.

You Are What You Read

BEANIE. Ask me something, anything, to do with asbestos – I know it all. It's a fibrous mineral, stretchy and soft but tough as hell. Word comes from the Ancient Greek meaning inextinguishable. Ancient Greeks loved the stuff – used to put their dead in asbestos shrouds to keep their ashes separate from the pyre.

I know about the cancer it causes too. The mesothelioma, the dyspnea, the metastasis...

I left school at sixteen for my first job in a laundrette. Worked with my hands all my life. Not just my bloody hands – my arms, my legs, my knees. Nobody wanted my brain. Finished school knowing three things – that I couldn't do maths, couldn't keep a fact in my head for history and couldn't understand science. That was shite, if you'll excuse my language. My brain's as good as anybody's.

That's why I decide not to take anyone with me to collect my X-ray results. You're supposed to have somebody there to ask the questions you're too dazed to ask. But I've been there and I don't want that for...

She looks at LUCY.

...People have busy lives.

LUCY. I'm doing the washing.

BEANIE. And I already know all the answers to the questions. I've spent the last five months with Jack learning everything.

JACK. What's the only thing worse than asbestos? Asworstos.

BEANIE. Thinks he's Billy bloody Connolly.

I'm on the bus to see Dr Sleeman. Woman opposite me is flicking through *Take a Break* while I'm dipping into a little light reading about carcinogens.

Biggest thing I've learnt is that intelligence is really just about what you're reading. A fact is a fact. Your brain uses the same technique whatever it is, creating new threads in your grey matter to bind it to your memory.

Doesn't matter whether it's that Lady Gaga believes she's being haunted by a ghost called Ryan or that there are six types of asbestos.

BEANIE *sings the names to the tune of 'Row, Row Your Boat'*.

Serpentine, amosite, crocidolite,
Tremolite, anthophyllite and actinolite.

I mean I'm not saying it's easy. When you're used to skimming through *Hello!*, it can be a bit of wrench:

BEANIE *reads from her book*.

'Asbestos fibres are phagocytised by the cells and when the cell undergoes mitosis, the fibres interfere with chromosome segregation which results in anaphase abnormalities.'

She lets that sit.

Phagocytised?! What the hell does that mean?

JACK. It's what bigots think happen if you shake hands with a queer fella, in't it?

BEANIE. Just means swallowed.

The cells want to protect the body from the fibres so they swallow them up. These things aren't so hard to understand so long as you've got a dictionary to hand and a bit of imagination. Imagine the cell is a washing machine.

Jack comes home with a dirty overall. I don't want to get my carpets mucky so I chuck the overalls in the machine. But this overall is so dirty, it clogs up the washing machine and stops it working properly.

Same with the fibres. They change the cells, actually change their DNA, so that they don't divide, grow and, if necessary, self-destruct the way healthy cells are supposed to.

My washing machine 'cell' is so buggered up by the overalls that it doesn't turn off and ends up flooding the whole damn house. My carpets, my machine, everything ruined because of Jack's dirty bloody overalls.

Guess Who Does All Her Washing?

LUCY. I'm doing the washing. I may not look like I am but I am.

She's not.

I can do this. Other people climb mountains, run marathons, parallel park, I can do the washing. I've done it before lots of times, I can do it now.

Ping.

A Facebook message saves me. From a girl I don't know any more but who used to be my best friend. She asks after me then writes an essay about her brilliant life with her two perfect children.

'David says hi.' David sodding Maxwell – her first and only boyfriend who used to chase us in the playground with his bogeys but who somehow has grown into this handsome hunk of a husband.

She tells me about her teaching job – primary – which is 'just soooo rewarding'. And in fact, that's why she's writing because she's looking for inspiring women to talk to her class about their jobs.

Inspiring women.

LUCY *lets this idea settle for a moment. She likes it.*

So I, an inspiring woman, ping a response back saying 'count me in'. And then, guess who does all her washing?

Not me. I can only manage one inspiring thing at a time.

Mesothelioma

BEANIE. 'Are you alright, Mrs Adamson? Is there somebody you want me to call?' I'm staring at the X-ray Dr Sleeman is holding. I don't need her to explain why there's fluid in my lungs or the irregular shapes attached to the membrane lining my chest. I don't need to hear her say mesothelioma. I know that word. I can even spell it.

'1898.'

'I'm sorry?' Dr Sleeman's looking at me, concerned.

'The year a factory inspector raised the alarm about asbestos. Ms L Deane Streatfield – she realised it was killing large numbers of textile workers.

1898, doctor. Seventy-three years before Jack walked into the shipyard with asbestos dust falling like snow.'

'Mrs Adamson, I know this is a lot to take in.'

'Took the American insurance companies a few more years to work it out but even they stopped selling life insurance to asbestos workers in 1918. That's... fifty-three years before Jack started working alongside the asbestos and not a mask to be had in the whole damn place. Even though they knew. Even though factory owners, shareholders, politicians... doctors – they all knew.'

A little embarrassed now, Dr Sleeman tells me she's made a referral and that I should prepare myself... and she doesn't say it but I know. Most people diagnosed with mesothelioma die within seven months.

I washed his overalls, you see. Jack's. They were never that bad. Only once or twice were they so dusty that I had to shake them down outside before scrubbing them in our kitchen sink, pulling them through the wringer and hanging them out to dry. Two times, maybe three. We were weans playing at 'wee hooses' – him in his first job and me trying to be a good wife with the washing – and now we're both dying.

PETE. I mean. Just shit. A really shit day.

A Mug's Game

JACK. I don't set much store by this 'could've, should've' stuff. There's any number of things we could've done or been.

PETE. Days like this. Any other job looks preferable.

JACK. A footballer or an astronaut.

PETE. Pencil-pusher, binman.

LUCY. Primary-school teacher – I could be good at that.

BEANIE. I could have been anything.

PETE. I could clean toilets for a living and I reckon I wouldn't have to deal with other people's shit as much as I do now.

JACK. It's a waste of time thinking about it. I started at the yards age sixteen, what you going to do? I'd have liked to be a comic like Billy Connolly – he worked the ships and all.

(*Best Billy Connolly impression.*) 'Never trust a man who, when left alone with a tea cosy, doesn't try it on.'

LUCY *laughs a little too loudly. Then, by way of explanation:*

LUCY. I've not been sleeping much lately.

PETE. Fucking comedians, the lot of them.

LUCY. Insomnia is awful. But on the plus side – only three more sleeps till Easter.

JACK. It was a friend of my uncle who fixed me up an apprenticeship with the UCS – Upper Clyde Shipbuilders. Good job, good people. I was to be a lagger's apprentice. Monkey-dung men, they called them. Cutting and fitting asbestos mattresses to insulate ships' pipes and boilers.

BEANIE. It doesn't burn you see. That's why they covered everything with it. It was supposed to save people's lives not take them.

PETE. Not asking them to kill themselves. A little bit of professionalism is all.

JACK. On my second day in the job, the dad of a girl I went to school with – he was a ship's electrician – tells me to watch out for that asbestos dust. So I ask my boss – a big man, jet-black hair that you only saw at the Barrowland dances because it was grey with dust the rest of the time. I ask him about the dust and he says, it's fine. It's the blue stuff, you've to watch out for.

This white stuff is fine. In fact, he has it on good authority from the doctor at the Turner & Newall factory where they make the stuff, that the magnesia in the dust is actually good for your stomach. 'Breathe it in, son,' he says, 'let that magnesia do its stuff.'

One again BEANIE *sings the names to the tune of 'Row, Row, Your Boat'.*

BEANIE. Serpentine, amosite, crocidolite,
Tremolite, anthophyllite and actinolite.

JACK. I asked if there were any masks and you could tell he thought I was pushing it.

'There's men welding over there, son, who've lost fingers doing their jobs, grateful they didn't lose a hand and you're worried about a bit of dust?'

He showed me where the masks were kept right enough. A box of them without filters, covered in asbestos.

I told the electrician what he'd said and he took me on the next day. I had to take a pay cut from an already small wage and we still worked around the dust but not in the same quantities, and when pals of mine started dying in the eighties and nineties, I thought it was the best decision I ever made to swap from the lagging to being an electrician.

JACK *has a coughing fit. Recovers himself.*

Thought I'd dodged a bullet.

PETE. 'Aye and pigs might fly.'

JACK. It's a mug's game. Regret. For years I thought I'd made the right decision shifting trade but now, if I wanted to dwell, I could say, well, the asbestos got me anyway, I should have stayed a bloody lagger, taken the extra wage over the years and had a couple more holidays, made more memories.

LUCY. Too many memories fizzing in my brain.

JACK. Thing is, I'm proud of the work I did. I've a flower from a bouquet sent by John Lennon and Yoko bloody Ono. How many people can say that?

Six months after I started at Scotstoun, the liquidators were sent in. Heath wouldn't give us a bail-out even though we'd have paid the Government back with plenty to spare soon as we'd finished the job. Heath says 'fuck you' and both Scotstoun and Clydebank yards are done in the same stroke. How we supposed to fight that? Picket lines, riots and the world hating us?

PETE. 'No, no fucking way.'

JACK. But Jimmy Airlie and Jimmy Reid weren't having that. They announce we're staging a 'work-in' to prove the yards are still viable. And God that man could speak. 'There will be no hooliganism, there will be no vandalism, and there will be no bevvying!' We kept our jobs. Sixteen months of taking charge of the yards and keeping management out.

PETE. You have to be prepared to be hated when you're a manager.

JACK. We worked our socks off and we showed them all. Working-class fucking heroes we were. The whole damn world was on our side. Love's young dream, John and Yoko, sent Jimmy a cheque to keep us going and an enormous bunch of roses. I made sure I nabbed me one. Beanie dried it in the airing cupboard for me. I keep it in a pot on the mantelpiece.

PETE. I'm four men down already because of Jamie's stag in Majorca. Whatever happened to a few bevvies in the pub the night before, for fuck's sake? Then this punk tells me he needs the day off because he needs 'study time'?

These union safety guys really take the piss. Officious little prick reminds me that I'm obliged to give him time off 'to keep abreast of changes in legislation'. Aye, right. Fucking duvet day more like.

You see this is why I keep my distance from my colleagues. Only time they'll ever see me out of hours is at the office party and even then, I'm gone soon as I've shown my face. Better that way. I'm their boss. They can't ask for favours or take the piss. It can be a wee bit lonely sometimes but it's worth it so I can say no with a clear conscience.

I can see he doesn't like it but I'm still surprised with what he comes out with then, this union safety little shit. 'You don't do nothing for nobody, do you, mate?'

PETE *absorbs that for a moment.*

'You don't know what I do and don't do for other people. One thing you can be sure I'll do, if you don't turn up tomorrow, is give you your fucking jotters.'

JACK. Part of my history, that is. And I'm not embarrassed to admit, I'm bloody proud of it.

PETE. 'Don't do nothing for nobody.'

PETE *laughs but it's got under his skin.*

PETE *shakes it off and tries* LUCY *on his mobile.*

(*Leaving a message.*) Lucy, it's Pete. You've not been responding to my emails. I need that wayleave for Hall Farm. Maybe you could call me?

LUCY. I just want to sleep.

Off the phone now...

PETE. I need that wayleave. We're due there at 9 a.m. Should be praying for snow. A hard icy field with six inches of snow is the only excuse they'll accept for not getting those cables laid tomorrow. But snow ain't forecast and I've learnt not to believe in miracles.

JACK. Proved bloody miracles can happen, that did. Would I have missed out on that? Not on your life. John bloody Lennon.

JACK *sings a little riff from John Lennon's 'Woman' about how he's sorry for causing her pain and sorrow and how he loves her.*

JACK *is looking straight at* BEANIE. *She meets his gaze, then, very deliberately, breaks it.*

Wayleaves and Easements

LUCY. 'I work for a small telecommunications company that works for a big telecommunications company and we lay fibre-optic cables! And my job is to organise the wayleaves and easements. A wayleave is an annual agreement with the landowner granting us permission to – because you see these cables travel for miles. I'm mean you could travel from here to the Southern Hemisphere with the lengths of cables we're laying. Whereas an easement is – well that's – because there's this network of fibre-optics... did I say that?'

Oh God, it's awful. I'm awful.

Inspiring? Only thing I'll inspire these kids to do is bunk off school.

I Will If You Will

BEANIE. Jack's gardening when I arrive home. Normally I'd go out and say, 'Slow down, mister. Don't tire yourself out.' But I don't today. I should do the ironing but I don't. I sit for ages, doing absolutely nothing, watching a moth flutter around the curtains.

JACK *approaches her.*

JACK. You're back. Thought you were just popping out for the messages? Started to worry about you.

BEANIE. –

JACK. You cross with me for gardening? Does me good. I got to keep working.

BEANIE. Your bloody 'work-in'.

JACK. Worked with Heath.

BEANIE. Heath wasn't a malignant bloody cancer.

JACK. He fucking was! You alright? Beanie?

BEANIE. My name's Dawn. Beanie's a stupid bloody name your granny gave me. I don't know why I've let you call me it all this time. It's a name thought up out of spite and I've worn it even though she's been dead these last thirty years.

JACK. Not out of spite.

BEANIE. Speaking in Gaelic when I was around to make me feel like an outsider. It's not even Beanie she was saying. It's Bean Nighe.

JACK. What you talking about?

BEANIE. She told me. Bumped into her on the bus about a year after we were married. She acted like she didn't know me. 'It's me, Granny – Beanie.' 'You've got it wrong, girl – Bean Nighe, not Beanie, Bean Nighe.' She spat it at me. 'The washerwoman, that's what you are, isn't it?'

JACK. 'Cause you worked in the laundrette.

BEANIE. Is that right? Innocent as that?

JACK. Course.

BEANIE. You're not minding the time I scared the life out of that old biddie from Skye. Came into the laundrette for the first time 'cause she was finding the steamie too tiring.

I told her she could trust me to do it right – why, even my own family call me 'Bean Nighe'. Blood drained from her face – she picked up her washing and fled the shop.

JACK. So?

BEANIE. Bean Nighe's a washerwoman alright, oh aye. She's often seen crouching by a stream or a loch washing clothes but she's washing them in blood and if you see her... you'd better say your prayers for death will follow soon.

Bean Nighe. She's an omen of death. Your bloody granny. She never did think I was good enough for you. I should have shoved her off that bus.

JACK. Ye cannae shove yir granny aff a bus.

A flicker of amusement crosses BEANIE*'s face but she's too cross to smile.* JACK *appeals to her...*

(*Singing.*) Oh, ye cannae shove yir granny aff a bus,
Oh, ye cannae shove yir granny –

BEANIE *can't resist.*

BEANIE (*singing*). 'Cause she's yir mammy's mammy –

JACK *and* BEANIE (*singing*). Oh, ye cannae shove yir granny aff a bus.

BEANIE (*sung*). Singing, I will if you will so will I –

(*Spoken, to* JACK.) Remember that bit.

JACK *and* BEANIE (*singing*). Singing, I will if you will so
　　will I,
　　Singing, I will if you will,
　　I will if you will,
　　I will if you will so will I.

　　They enjoyed that but it's over now.

BEANIE. I was at the doctor's. My X-ray results.

JACK. What she say? What's on the X-rays? Beanie?

BEANIE. Looks like it's a case of I will if you will so will I.

　　This news hits JACK *hard. He walks away.*

　　Jack. Jack, come back and talk to me about it. Jack.

Jack's Routine

JACK. Have you heard the one about the fella who died of
　　asbestos? Took 'em three days to burn him.

　　So I just heard my wife's got mesothelioma. Mesothelioma
　　jokes are hard to write but I'm trying asbestos I can,
　　amirite?! Turns out I poisoned her but hell, that just makes us
　　even, have you tried her spaghetti Bolognese?

BEANIE. Jack.

JACK. No, no, I'm kidding on. I was devastated when she told
　　me. When she said I made her breathless, that isn't what
　　I thought she meant. So that's two of us now suffering from
　　the same affliction – I'm not talking about mesothelioma,
　　I'm talking about marriage.

BEANIE. Talk to me, Jack.

JACK. She's raging about it. Threatening to beat me to death.
　　Not with her fists. Just she might die first. When I got my
　　diagnosis, doctor told me I'd only seven months to live.
　　I asked him, 'Is there nothing I can do?' 'Aye, you can marry

an accountant and move to Paisley.' 'Will that extend my
life, doctor?' 'No, but it'll make the seven months you have
left seem much longer.'

BEANIE. Talk to me. You never bloody talk to me.

JACK. I'm not afraid to die, I just don't want to be there when
it happens. And I don't care if people don't say nice things
about me at the funeral. Only thing I want them to say is,
'Look, he's moving.'

BEANIE. Forget it.

JACK. I feel like somebody has wrapped my heart in plastic
and they keep twisting it tighter and tighter.

But BEANIE *has already stopped listening.*

Don't Do Nothing for Nobody

PETE. 'Don't do nothing for nobody.'

He's got me thinking about Mum, now.

There's a look a woman gives to a guy. Disappointment.

I grew up seeing my mum give that look. To my dad. Not to
me. I made sure of that. But...

Last time I saw her. Sitting in her favourite faded grey
armchair, still weak from a bout of pneumonia. It was there
in her eyes. Glassy-eyed and frightened. Not of death but
that she'd taught me the wrong lessons.

Bean Nighe

LUCY. I'm doing the washing! Old-style though in a metal tub. Scrubbing at the stains, really getting my elbow into it like some tough old biddie at the steamie. This is how to wash clothes. I pull out my top, a pretty white blouse with lace butterflies on it and I wring out the liquid. But it's not water that comes out. I'm washing the clothes in blood.

LUCY wakes with a gasp from a bad dream. Takes a moment to steady her breathing.

PETE. Some images you just need to forget.

LUCY. Just a bad dream.

PETE. Shake it off.

An Invisible Web of Fibres

LUCY has a ball of red wool that she's winding round various objects as a visual aid for her presentation.

LUCY. 'There are fibre-optic cables everywhere, beneath your feet, an underground web of fibres binding us all to each other, connecting us so we need never feel alone again.

And through these fibres, you can watch *Rainbow* or *ThunderCats* or…' a programme that's actually made this decade. *Teletubbies*? Check programmes.

She makes a note on her 'script' for the presentation. Her phone rings.

Pete Harris. Second time he's called. Awkward. Can't deal with you now.

She rejects the call, finishes taking her note. The answer-machine notification buzzes.

'There are fibre-optic cables everywhere, beneath your feet, an underground' no, invisible. Invisible is better.

' – an invisible web of fibres binding us all to each other – '

The phone rings again.

I said, not now.

She answers it by accident.

Fuck.

PETE. Lucy.

LUCY. Pete, hi.

PETE. You said you'd send me the Hall Farm wayleave days ago.

LUCY. I did.

PETE. You didn't.

LUCY. No, I didn't yet but I did… say I would.

PETE. You're not in the office…

LUCY. I'm working from home on a presentation for this afternoon. A big presentation for…

She realises the seven-year-olds aren't a good enough excuse.

Shareholders! *Future* shareholders.

PETE. We're laying cables there at 9 a.m. tomorrow morning. Get it sent! Or do I need to head over to your place and stand over you while you email it?

LUCY *bristles at this.*

LUCY. Course not. I'll put it in the Dropbox straight away in a folder marked 'Keep Your Pants On' or would you rather I emailed it to you? Subject heading 'There's no need to be a dick'?

This disarms PETE.

PETE. Suppose that's fair.

LUCY. I'll send it now.

PETE. Good. Thanks.

LUCY. You don't know where I live anyway.

PETE. I do actually. Opposite the leisure centre.

LUCY. There's thirty flats opposite the leisure centre…

PETE. But yours is the one with the green door and stained-glass window above the close.

LUCY. You've been?

PETE. No! Look, I'm not stalking you or anything. You told me.

LUCY. I never told you.

PETE. You did. At the office party.

Gulp – that party…

LUCY. Oh.

PETE. You said the weekend began for you when you closed your green door behind you and stood for five minutes with the colours from the stained glass shining on your face.

LUCY. I'd forgotten I'd said that.

PETE. It was right before you…

LUCY. Threw a snowball in your face and ran away.

PETE. Yeah.

LUCY. That was nearly a year ago. You must have a photographic memory or something.

PETE. Well it was a conversation, not a thing so photographic's not… I liked the thought of it. I remembered. That's all.

An awkward silence.

Look, send me the wayleave and I won't step near your green door, okay.

LUCY. Okay.

PETE. Okay.

Thank you.

Sorry I was a dick.

LUCY. Yeah. Well, I'd better –

PETE. Good luck with your big presentation.

LUCY. Thanks. It's going to be good I think. I'm doing this thing with wool. It's like a visual aid so…

PETE. Send me that email.

LUCY. Sending it now.

LUCY puts down the phone, take a few breaths to recover from the call.

Right. Wayleave. Wayleave, wayleave.

She goes over to her laptop.

Postman Pat, is that too young for seven-year-olds?

Typing into Google:

Programmes for seven-year-olds – *Ninjago*. That sounds cool. I'll use that. 'And through this little fibre, you can watch… *Ninjaaaaaaaaaago*.'

Yeah, she likes how that sounds.

Malignant Seeding

BEANIE. We don't speak much after. A few grunts about everyday stuff. Nothing you could call a conversation. I don't tell anybody else either.

BEANIE *looks at* LUCY.

I'm just not ready. Next time I empty Jack's chest-drain I see the beginnings of a lump by the catheter. The consultant told us to look out for this. It's called malignant seeding. That lump is the mesothelioma. It has travelled along the tract made by the needle from his lung until it has hit the underside of the skin. Like it's trying to burst out and get me. Jack's cancer is showing me it is there, like an alien baby pushing out of the chest of that Sigourney Weaver.

Hello, cancer.

I put my finger on it and push it back into Jack's body. Jack yelps in pain. I squeeze harder.

Go away. Leave me alone.

Spiky and Difficult

LUCY. My friend meets me outside the school office. She is warm and effortless and I feel even more awkward. I ask about her kids and she tells me a witty anecdote about each one. She asks me how my parents are but I don't have any funny anecdotes about them. Talking about them would be the opposite of warm and effortless. It would be spiky and difficult and I would probably cry. So I say a sort of vague 'yeah' and ask after hers. They are well, on a cruise in the Caribbean as we speak. Lucky things, I say. And I ask about David Maxwell. And she teases me for still calling him by his full name.

'We're not at school now, Lucy.'

'We are!' I say and we laugh and she walks me into a classroom full of bright-eyed expectant seven-year-olds and I. Am. Terrified.

Dirty and Contaminated

BEANIE. I've been a good nurse to Jack. Attentive, gentle, meticulous. I surprised myself. Maybe I should have been a nurse. Scrap that, I should've been a fucking surgeon. The things I could have done. I'm so full of... [regret.]

We have moths in our home. I've seen them around for months but it's only now I realise that they have been burying their way into the fibres in our carpets, our sofa, our clothes. I pull out the clothes at the back of the rail.

Jack's wedding suit – he's not worn it for years of course – but now it's riddled with holes. Those bastards have chewed through the wool. My woollen skirt is hanging next to it and I think:

'Don't you dare. Don't you dare have crawled off Jack's suit onto my skirt.'

When I look, there doesn't seem to be any holes so I'm relieved until I spot something at the bottom when I'm hanging it back up.

It's a... worm, larvae, maggotty little thing and it's on my skirt and everything is dirty and contaminated and I feel so...

I kill five moths on my way down the stairs. I squish them dead with the same finger I squished Jack's lump. Their squished dead bodies smeared on our white walls with a smudge of grey dust and as disgusting as it is, I feel a sense of satisfaction when I walk past them.

A Fucking Pyre

PETE. She hasn't sent it.

Why am I even surprised? That's what people do, isn't it? My dad always let my mum down. Like gravity.

Always had an excuse, always claimed to be helping somebody else. Nearly missed my birth because he was helping our elderly neighbour paint his house. Helping him empty his whisky supplies while he was at it no doubt. Mum and he lost out on their dream house because my dad lent the deposit money to a drinking pal of his who never paid him back. Cost Dad his marriage, that did. Christmas Eve and he's out drinking with the aforementioned pal. Mum flips and sets fire to a load of my dad's stuff in the garden. A fuck-off huge blaze.

I was desperate for snow that Christmas. Instead, I got bonfire ash floating around my bedroom window and the sounds of them screaming at each other. A neighbour telling them to quieten down and put out the fire – you're not allowed bonfires in the city. Mum screams back:

'It's not a bonfire, it's a fucking pyre.'

Hate and More Hate

BEANIE. Something's changed in Jack since he heard my
diagnosis. He's stopped going for walks, he rarely steps
outside. And something's changed in me too. I don't want to
play nurse any more. I'm tired and every task I do to make
Jack more comfortable, I find myself thinking – you won't
be doing this for me.

I see him struggling and I don't help. I'm on strike. I used to
be gentle and give him space and time, now I tut at him. I tut
a lot.

JACK. Beanie?

BEANIE. We can both feel the distance between us.

PETE. It was their marriage she was burning. It was a fucking
funeral.

JACK. Dawn? Sweetheart?

BEANIE. It's always been there but I'm not bothering to hide it
any more.

She looks at him, her eyes full of hate.

Jack turned me into this. I was a healthy cell, lots of
potential, until I took him on. He changed me, changed my
DNA. He made me hard, he made me petty and mean and
resentful and I don't know how to make all that hate self-
destruct. So I just let it grow and grow.

JACK. Beanie!

Hate and more hate.

BEANIE. I married a carcinogen and this is what he's turned
me in to.

PETE. Life gives you ash when you're expecting snow.

Pericardial Problems

BEANIE. When we next see Jack's consultant, he's worried
from the off. Says he can see a marked different in Jack's
appearance. He does look grey, more hunched. He looks
terrible. The consultant orders more X-rays then and there.

He's very thorough. The oncology doctors in Glasgow are
first rate.

So they bloody should be. Scotland has the highest incidence
of mesothelioma in the world.

The results are not good. He has developed pericardial
mesothelioma. The cancer has moved. It's on his heart now.
A layer of cancer is encasing his heart like cling film.

JACK. Doctor doctor, can I have a second opinion? Of course.
Come back tomorrow.

The Presentation

LUCY. It starts brilliantly. I go round the group asking them to
tell me what they want to be when they grow up. I don't
want to just talk at them, I want to show them I'm interested
in them. I'd have made a great teacher. Maybe I should
retrain? Anyway, it's the usual stuff, 'I want to be a builder',
'I want to be a singer', 'I want to be a 3D graphics
engineer?' Okay so that one's a bit niche. There's this one
kid I really don't like the look of. He's got one of those
punchable faces. Sorry but he does. Piggy eyes, smug smile
and he keeps kicking the girl in front but he's clever about it
and makes sure the staff don't see. He sees me clock it and
smiles – what are you going to do about it?! The little shit
wants to be Prime Minister. Figures. So then I launch in on
my presentation and it's all going swimmingly until Piggy-
Eyes interrupts – 'Miss, are you married?' No, no, I'm not.
'Do you have a boyfriend?' No. 'Why not?'

LUCY *tries to answer that one. She's forming the words but somehow no answer seems right so she doesn't follow through.*

All the while he's kicking the girl in front absentmindedly. I ignore him and continue with my presentation.

'...so the internet isn't just magic, even though it might seem it, it's travelling along...'

Now he's flicking the girl in the back of the head. It's really distracting. Come on, Lucy. You're a professional.

'...all these cables into a unit in your home and when you get back tonight I want you to ask all your mummies and daddies to show you...'

Smiling and flicking.

She drops her presentation notes. She scrabbles about to pick them up but they are all out of order.

Oh no. Damn it.

'Whoopsie. Never mind. I don't need them. Where was I?'

A dangerously cute girl on the front row with pigtails like I used to have says, 'mummies and daddies'.

'Mummies and daddies. Yes. That's right. Mummies and daddies.' Mummies and daddies.

Poison in Our Home

BEANIE *and* JACK *sink into two seats, set back to back. They are on a bus.*

BEANIE. We don't say a word on the bus home from the consultant. I ding the bell and get up from my seat and he catches my arm.

JACK. Do you wish you hadn't married me?

BEANIE. Why are you asking me that?

JACK. Because I brought poison into our home. I poisoned you.

BEANIE. Did you?

Maybe a little, when you bought me tatty garage-shop flowers for our first wedding anniversary. Or when you watched me do the ironing from the comfort of your big armchair when I'd been on my feet all day.

You poisoned me when you refused to talk about the miscarriages.

And when you insisted we go to your mother's for Christmas lunch when I'd lost the baby only two days before. And when it was my first Mother's Day with Lucy and you didn't give me a card.

You poisoned me when you stopped kissing me hello and took a cuddle from Lucy instead. And when you stopped touching me. And when you were too slow to say you didn't mind my body getting old. And when you watched me settle for less than I could be.

The dust you brought home, hell, Jack, that wasn't even your fault. But I don't say any of that. I just say.

'Come on, we'll miss our stop.'

Mummies and Daddies

LUCY. 'Mummies and daddies. Yes. That's right. Mummies and Daddies...

I used to have a mummy and daddy when I was your age. Nine months ago I had a mummy and a daddy. Now I don't have either.

Are you smiling? Yes, you, with the eyes.

You'll make a brilliant Prime Minister because you... you like hurting people – I've seen you flicking that poor wee girl – and that's first in the job description if you're running things.

Hurting people. You'll have to be good at maths too. People like you made money from exposing my dad to poison. Knowing it would kill them. Knowing that if they employed the right lawyers and strung out the legal stuff until after the workers died, it wouldn't make too much of a dent in their profits. They did the maths – it was cheaper to let them die. No, hold on please, Mrs Maxwell. Let me finish.

I can make them pay now. But how much? Don't just look at me. I'm asking you. You, with the pigtails. How much is your daddy worth? A hundred and fifty thousand pounds? A hundred and eighty thousand pounds? What about your mummy? Are mummies worth more? How much money can make up for the fact they took my mummy from me?'

And I'm crying now. Sobbing my heart out. And most of the kids are crying too. And that feels… quite nice actually. Because I didn't cry at Mum's funeral. She didn't cry at Dad's and at hers I knew why. Because you don't get to cry when you're the adult. So while I don't feel great about making a bunch of seven-year-olds cry, I'm sort of glad I have.

The little girl with pigtails is pretty hysterical by now and the teaching assistant is trying to calm her down. Piggy-Eyes isn't crying. Of course not. But I definitely wiped the smile off his face.

And my used-to-be-a-friend is walking towards me, furious.

But I don't want to finish yet. I didn't even get to do the thing with the wool.

Marriage is Colder than Snow

BEANIE. It's snowing outside when Lucy lets herself in. Jack and me haven't spoken since we got off the bus. I'm ironing. He's just sitting. Shrunken and grey. A moth has landed on his arm and he doesn't even bat it away.

LUCY. I just hit a colleague in the face.

BEANIE. Hello, Lucy.

LUCY. With a snowball. Not my fist.

BEANIE. Why did you do that?

LUCY. Doesn't matter. Alright, Dad.

JACK *looks up but doesn't respond.*

How did it go with the consultant?

Neither of them respond.

Is something wrong?

BEANIE. No, love.

JACK. Tell her.

BEANIE. She doesn't need to –

JACK. Tell her.

LUCY. Tell me what? Will you stop ironing Dad's pants for one minute and tell me what's going on.

BEANIE. You tell her.

JACK. I will if you will so will I.

LUCY. Will somebody please tell me what's going on?

BEANIE. Your father's cancer has moved to his heart.

JACK. Your mother's got it too. From washing my overalls. She breathed in my cancer.

LUCY *looks from one to the other, in shock.*

In for a Penny, in for a Pound

LUCY. 'Lucy, it's finished,' she spits out at me in a raspy
whisper. Nothing warm or effortless about her now. And
she's gripping my wrist tightly with one hand while the other
pushes hard into the small of my back. And she walks me
past the class, past Piggy-Eyes and I glare at him and I say:

'Do you want to know why I don't have a husband? Because
marriage is poisonous. Don't let anybody tell you different.

Girls, if you look deep into Mrs Maxwell's eyes, you'll see
what years of washing and ironing a man's pants will do to
you. Take it from me – loneliness sucks but at least there's
nobody dragging you fucking down.'

In for a penny, in for a pound. Maybe teaching's not for me
after all.

Send the Fucking Wayleave

PETE *is on the phone leaving* LUCY *a message.*

PETE. Lucy. It's Pete. You've not sent it. You said you'd send
it. I need it first thing tomorrow morning and it's now five
fifty-eight and. Please send me the wayleave. Please send it
to me. Please.

PETE *hangs up. Has a little angry burst of frustration where
he nearly throws his phone to the ground but manages to
restrain himself.*

Brandy in the Grand Hall

JACK *is holding a dried rose.*

JACK. We've done it. Kicked the managers out and showed the
world how Glasgow makes ships. We've built an enormous
cruise ship and we've sprayed it everywhere with asbestos so
all who sail in her will be safe from fire. The kings and
queens will be safe, the titled and the wealthy will sail the
seas eating caviar and they'll all be safe. Bravo! And the best
bit is we'll get to keep our jobs… for a decade more, at least.
Another ten years of breathing in poisonous dust, taking it
home to our wives and weans. All for less wages each year
than the rich passengers spend on brandy in the grand hall
we built. We did it.

We did it.

JACK *crumbles the rose to dust in his hands and blows it
away.*

Nostalgia isn't what it used to be.

Tethered Together

PETE. Doesn't matter how low I set the bar of expectation,
people always manage to crawl below it.

Is she trying to punish me? 'Cause I went to kiss her at the
Christmas party? That was a year ago! And anyway, she
leaned in first.

I wasn't looking to pull at a work do. Not my style at all.
I was making a getaway when I see her hanging about
outside. And we start to talk. It was easy with her.
Comfortable. And when it started to snow, it just felt… And
she's looking up at me like I'm Cary Grant and then
something clouds over and she's shoving ice in my face.
What changed her mind? What did she see in me that scared
her off?

I don't get women. I know you're not supposed to… generalise like… but, I just don't.

I took Mum's side in the split. She was right, Dad was a prick. And when he died, I was mostly pissed off that his funeral clashed with a big climbing event I was competing in. But Mum – she was in pieces. I'd hated him all these years because she did and now she tells me there's a cord joining her and him that can't ever be broken. Just like with my rock-climbing. She and my dad climbing on different rock faces but tethered together, there for each other if one of them should fall.

'You cut the cord, Mum. Dad was dragging you down and you cast him lose.'

She said she didn't. She wanted to but she just couldn't. Why not? And she says – I remember it so clearly – she says:

'Because then who would have caught me if I'd fallen?'

Me. I would. Fucking women.

Falling

LUCY *is home. Her phone rings. She rejects the call.*

LUCY. Not now, Pete Harris.

She dials a number on speed dial. We hear BEANIE*'s voicemail message. 'Hi, this is Beanie, leave me a message.' Beep.*

Mum, it's me. Lucy. I just wanted to hear your voice. I'm so tired. If you gave me a penny for my thoughts, you'd get change. My place is a mess. You'd be raging if you saw it.

Bags of yours and Dad's stuff everywhere, muddled up with mine. I haven't washed anything, not a thing since… And moths are everywhere.

These tiny little dusty grey things. Everything feels dirty but I can't bring myself to… It's like a… block or something. That and sleeping. Little things ordinary people do. Feel. Impossible. There's so many letters. You'd know what to tell the lawyers. I just can't face it. Maybe if I could just get one good night's sleep. I can only manage a few minutes here and there when other people are around – on the bus, in a café. I'm actually frightened of lying down. That sick terribly lonely feeling lurches up in me when I close my eyes, like I'm falling. If I could hear your voicemail on a loop, I think maybe I might manage a few minutes of –

BEEP. Voicemail cuts her off. She sits clutching the phone. Exhausted.

Bear Hugs

PETE. I miss her.

That thing she did burning Dad's stuff. She wasn't like that usually. Never seen her do anything like it before or since. Fucking terrified me. Worst night of my life. Anytime I feel low, lonely, I'm back there in my head.

Mum was quiet. Didn't show her emotions. Dad was a soppy fucker but Mum… not sure I can even remember her saying the words 'I love you'. But I knew I was loved. Could smell it in the banana bread she made on Fridays and the way she puffed up the pillows on my bed. She'd fold my socks in this special way so you could pull them on easier. Even when I'd left home. She had a key to my place and I'd come home to find these beautiful piles of washed, ironed and perfectly folded clothes. She wasn't a toucher either, my mum. But those neat piles were like bear hugs.

Home Visit

LUCY. Pete?

PETE. Hall Farm wayleave.

LUCY. Oh God, I'm sorry.

PETE. I have phoned you nineteen times in the last hour. The last three, I was standing on the street outside, willing you to answer so I wouldn't have to do this. Ta-dah! Arrive on your doorstep like some sort of freak but you left me with no choice.

LUCY. Sorry. Sorry. Sorry, sorry, sorry.

PETE. It's fine. Just. Just send me the wayleave.

LUCY. I will. I'm sorry. I'm really sorry.

PETE. Don't be sorry. Just send me the email.

LUCY. Of course. Okay, I'll do it straight away. I'm so sorry you had to come all the way here.

PETE. If you could send it while I'm here, I'd be happier. Because you've said you'll send it and then not. So I'm thinking I won't leave until I actually have it on my phone. Sorry if that sounds… threatening or. Just to be sure.

LUCY. No I totally understand.

LUCY *opens her laptop, finds the wayleave in her documents.*

Hall Farm, Hall Farm.

PETE. You do have it, don't you?

LUCY. Yes. Here it is – look.

PETE. Okay. Good.

LUCY. I'm sending it to you now. See. There it is attached.

PETE. Okay.

LUCY. Done.

PETE. Thank you.

LUCY. Is that it then? It's just I was about to go to sleep.

PETE. It's only seven o'clock.

LUCY. I haven't been sleeping very…

PETE. Yeah, you look awful.

LUCY. Okay.

PETE. Really tired, I mean. You don't look awful. Don't think you ever could. I'm just going to wait until the email's on my phone and then I'll. Leave.

LUCY. Has it not come through yet?

PETE. Nope.

LUCY. It's on its way.

PETE. I know.

LUCY. It's travelling along metres and metres of fibre as we speak. An invisible fibre linking you and me. Sorry, I'm talking… I'm really tired. Do you want to sit down?

PETE. Okay.

There's nowhere to sit down. Bags of clothes are everywhere, clothes toppling out of the bags. PETE picks up a pair of man's trousers, then a very dated woman's blouse.

You a secret jumble-sale junkie?

LUCY. No. They belong to my. My parents.

PETE. Oh, sorry. Are they…?

LUCY. They died. Said that out loud for the first time today. Middle of my presentation, broke down and cried.

PETE. In front of the shareholders?

LUCY. A group of seven-year-olds. I sort of fudged the whole shareholder thing.

PETE. Oh well that's a relief. Seven-year-olds?

LUCY. Yeah. Made the whole class cry.

PETE. Oh.

LUCY. I don't think they'll be asking me back.

PETE. No.

When did they…?

LUCY. Dad died nine months ago. Mum ten weeks.

PETE. Fucking hell.

LUCY. Yeah.

PETE. How?

LUCY. I'm not going to. I'd rather not. Talk about them actually.

PETE. Okay.

An awkward silence.

Shouldn't you take these to the charity or… Maybe you're not ready…?

LUCY. It's not that. My parents had moths so. There's like larva in some of them and I don't want to infect a charity shop. And I don't want to just bin them because there's some nice things in there and. I just need to sort them.

Throw out anything with holes.

Wash the rest, make sure they're not… infected or anything. Thing is I'm. I've not been able to do any clothes-washing for a while.

PETE. Is your machine broken?

LUCY. No, it's fine. It's me. I. It's a silly thing. It's one of those jobs you wish you could click your fingers and it all be done.

PETE. I got loads of those.

LUCY. Yeah. I'm thinking about building a giant bonfire and just burning the whole lot.

PETE. Don't do that.

LUCY *is a little unnerved by* PETE*'s earnestness.*

LUCY. Apparently the Romans used to weave asbestos fibres into their cloths and then to clean them, they'd just chuck them in fire. The cloths came out whiter than when they went in.

PETE. Not sure that would work on these.

LUCY. No. It's just something my mum told me.

I'm so tired. I keep having this bad dream. I'm scrubbing clothes in a... and when I take them out I see I've been washing them in... Sorry. You don't want to know all this. Has the message not arrived yet?

PETE *looks at his phone.*

PETE. No. Not yet.

(*To the audience.*) That's a lie. 'No' just feels like the right answer somehow.

LUCY. It's a really horrible dream. It's not so bad if I sleep around other people in like a café or... because there's bustle to calm me down when I wake up but I do get quite a few weird looks. Maybe I dribble or snore or shout out in my sleep. I don't know. I'm so tired.

A moment. LUCY's exhaustion is apparent.

PETE. Would it help if I stayed a while? While you sleep. So you're not alone.

LUCY. That's a bit...

PETE. Yeah, I know.

LUCY. 'Cause it's not like –

PETE. No. I know. Of course. It was a weird –

LUCY. Yeah, pretty weird.

PETE. Don't know why I –

LUCY (*with sudden urgency*). It might help.

PETE. Sorry?

LUCY. I mean... it's worth a try isn't it?

PETE. Oh. Yeah.

LUCY. Even if I just managed ten minutes or...

PETE. Yeah.

LUCY. So you would be happy to –

PETE. Sure.

LUCY. And you wouldn't leave?

PETE. Not if you don't want me to.

LUCY. You'll stay till I wake?

PETE. If that's what you want.

LUCY. Just an hour or so and then I could order us some takeaway for dinner to say thank you?

Say yes.

PETE. Yes.

LUCY. Okay. Okay, thank you. Thank you! And you really won't leave?

PETE. I'll be here when you wake.

PETE *smiles at her reassuringly.*

I'll Catch You

PETE*'s smile drops when it dawns on him what he's offered. He's got to sit here surrounded by moth-eaten clothes waiting for a girl he doesn't know to wake up.*

PETE. I'd forgotten about the match. When I offered. Or maybe, I'd remembered in the back of my mind but I suppose I thought I could just watch it on her telly but it turns out she doesn't have one. Not in the lounge anyway and I don't have enough battery to watch it (because I've spent the whole day phoning her) so now I'm sitting in her messy flat, trying not to make any noise and missing the fucking match. I'm such a mug.

I'm going to go. I know I said I'd stay but I've been here an hour and if knowing I was here helped her to get to sleep, then I've done my bit already. I mean what am I going to do if she wakes up frightened from her dream? I don't know what to say. I'm shit at that stuff.

'Don't do nothing for nobody.'

Mum, sitting in her grey armchair, wanting to talk to me about my dad. Telling me he was a good man deep down. 'Dad wasn't a good man.' I say. 'A good man looks after his own. Family first, fuck everybody else.' 'And what if somebody has no family?' She asks. 'Can you still be a good man if you do nothing for nobody?' That look. The one she reserved for my dad. Disappointment. I shake it off. 'I got family. I got you.' And her eyes go all glassy then. She must have known. That I wouldn't have family for long. She died in her sleep two nights later.

Lucy isn't family. There's no cord tying me to her. I'm going.

And I'm at the door. And I'm not looking back. But underneath my coat, there's a huge pile of letters. Legal letters mostly about her parents, photocopies and a ton of articles printed from the internet.

PETE *picks up the papers, can't help himself but read. He begins to get a picture of what has happened to* LUCY*'s parents.*

Fucking hell.

PETE *decides to stay.*

I start to sort through the pile of clothes in Lucy's living room. I pull out and bin anything that's moth-damaged and I sort the rest into lights and darks and I wash the clothes. All the clothes. Some I hang on radiators, others I tumble-dry and then I iron them in batches and place them in neat piles around the room. And the hours pass and now I don't want her to wake up because I want to get it done and I'm getting through it all and I'm ironing the last pile and I get to a top that's clearly Lucy's not her mum's and I iron it really carefully and it's pretty much done but I take a little longer on it and I think...

I'll catch you, Lucy. I'll catch you.

But if I'm honest, really fucking honest, I wonder if maybe I'm the one that's falling and I'm doing this so that Lucy will catch me.

The Conversation

Out of time and space. A conversation they could and should have had.

JACK. I'm sorry.

BEANIE. Stop it. There's a lot of people who should say sorry before you, Jack. The people who lined their pockets with the money off it, the people who kept quiet when they should have spoken up. Stop saying sorry.

JACK. Not for that. For not talking to you about the miscarriages.

BEANIE. Oh.

Yeah, we should have talked about that.

JACK. We could now.

BEANIE. I suppose we could.

JACK. Were they boys or girls, do you think?

BEANIE. A wee girl, the first one I think.

JACK. What would we have called her?

BEANIE. I don't know. I didn't let myself.

JACK. Lydia.

BEANIE. That's nice. Yes. Lydia.

JACK. And the second one?

BEANIE. I felt sure he was a wee boy.

JACK. William. After your da.

BEANIE. Jack, I thought. I thought we would call him Jack.

JACK. I'd have liked that.

BEANIE. They'd have been alive when you were coming home in your dusty overalls. I've read of people dying now because they gave their daddies a hug when they came home from work when they were weans. I couldn't have borne it if that dust had poisoned our babies.

JACK. It would have crushed me.

BEANIE. I know it would. I felt like my world was torn apart when we lost them and I could never think there'd be a day when I'd be glad those little babes didn't survive. But things look different from different angles, don't they.

Lucy coming later, missed the years you were at the ships, and so something that was full of heartache, feels like it was the right thing now.

JACK. You see regret's a mug's game.

BEANIE. You always said that. That's why I was so surprised. That time you asked me if I wished I'd not married you. Wasn't like you.

JACK. Surprised myself with that one.

BEANIE. Do you wish you'd not married me?

JACK. Course I bloody don't.

And you? Do you wish you'd never said 'I do'.

BEANIE. I didn't say 'I do' – only say that in the movies, or in America anyway. Scottish service you say 'I will' or have you forgotten?

JACK. You're avoiding the question.

BEANIE. I thought I did. I spent years thinking I gave more than I got in our marriage. But we'd been together so long I didn't know where I ended and you began. We were so wrapped up in each other, I used to feel I couldn't breathe but I'll tell you something, Jack, when they took out part of my lung, it didn't hurt as much as it did when I lost you. All those threads tying us together had been keeping me safe all this time and I never knew it.

JACK. What do you call a woman with only half a lung?
Breathless.

BEANIE. Don't.

JACK. My wife had the left side of her body removed by
doctors – she's all *right* now.

BEANIE. Jack!

JACK. What do you call your wife when she loses both her
eyes? No eye dear.

BEANIE. Stop it.

JACK. Alright, alright.

I was right all these years about regret. It is the way it is.
That's your lot and you should accept it not wish it undone.
Even the asbestos. We might never have realised how much
we loved each other without it.

BEANIE. No. No, love. They stole years from us. The people
responsible, those that were making money off it and those
that let it happen, doctors who didn't speak out, politicians
who let it pass. It's on all of them and you should never
forget it.

JACK. Sixty-four wasn't such a bad innings.

BEANIE. Don't be so Scottish, Jack. Low expectations have
been bred into us from birth. Living into your seventies and
eighties doesn't have to be just for them born with silver
spoons in their mouths. Years we could have lived and loved
each other, could have watched Lucy become all she can be.
They stole that from us and we can never stop being angry
about that. Never.

JACK. You're right.

BEANIE. I hope our dying doesn't scar her. Lucy. I want her
to be open and happy and free of it. She can't let it poison
her too.

LUCY. I won't, Mum.

LUCY *has watched the whole thing. She has seen her parents' marriage clearly for the first time. It wasn't just poison they shared. It was love.*

JACK. Hello, love.

BEANIE. I didn't know you were there.

LUCY. I'm here.

BEANIE. You look tired.

LUCY. I'm a fuck-up.

JACK. You are not.

LUCY. I haven't been coping without you. All the legal stuff. I could fill a coffin with unanswered legal letters. I'm a total fuck-up.

BEANIE. Well don't be.

LUCY. They want me to come up with a number. For Dad's compensation and for yours. How much shall I say, Dad? Mum? How much were you worth?

They can't answer.

I don't want the money. I want you. Can I just tell the lawyers that?

JACK. Course you can.

BEANIE. No.

They knew it would kill us but instead of making people's places of work safe, they paid the paltry fines – as little as twenty-five pounds in some cases for exceeding safe limits of asbestos in the air. Fifty men at a time breathing in poisonous dust, each of them dying twenty years earlier than they should – that's a thousand years in just one workplace. And that's not counting their poor wives and weans who hugged them when they got home from work. A fine of twenty-five pounds for stealing over a thousand years?

They put profit over life. So you think of a number and double it. Chip away at their bonuses, their nest eggs, their private health care, their retirement cruises. Make our deaths cost them, love. You hear me.

LUCY. Okay. Okay, I will.

I've got so many things I want to ask you... oh, oh, I think I'm going to wake up now. I'm bursting for a pee.

Will I see you again? Will I?

Snow

LUCY *wakes up.*

PETE. Hello.

LUCY. You stayed.

PETE. I stayed.

LUCY. Are we having dinner?

PETE. Breakfast.

LUCY. Breakfast?! You stayed all night.

PETE. I stayed. Come on, I'll take you to that café down the road. My treat. And then I've got to lay some fibre-optic through –

LUCY. Hall Farm.

I follow Pete into my living room. I think it's mine but it's totally transformed, maybe I'm still dreaming. All my clothes are washed and ironed and in perfect piles. My mum's and dad's too. I pick up a jumper my dad wore on Sundays and stroke my fingers over every fibre of wool. I do the same with a cotton summer dress my mum wore on my eighteenth birthday. I hold them both to me and for just a moment I feel like I'm hugging them both again. A great big bear hug. I look at Pete and I feel like a layer of plastic around my heart is melting.

LUCY *looks at* PETE, *overwhelmed.*

PETE. Come on.

LUCY. We walk out of my flat, out of my close and onto the road and –

Snow begins to fall on them all.

JACK. Bloody hell.

BEANIE. Well I –

LUCY. Pete, look –

PETE *and* LUCY. Snow!

LUCY. And he looks like he's seven years old. We both do. Wide-eyed, full of joy at this moment. And suddenly our eyes are on each other and I'm leaning in and we're going to kiss, lovers in our own black-and-white film and –

PETE. You're not going to thrust a handful of ice in my face?

LUCY. No. Not this time.

Relieved, PETE *goes in for the kiss but just before he does, his phone rings. Totally killing the moment.*

Oh.

PETE. Sorry.

PETE answers the phone.

Yep.

LUCY. You're taking it? Okay.

PETE (*into the phone*). Are you telling me or asking me?

…

Even though I said I'd sack you if you took it?

PETE *looks at* LUCY. *She changes everything for him.*

Well none of us was counting on snow… Aye, alright. You take your duvet day.

He hangs up.

Sorry about that. Union-safety joker just grew a pair. Where were we?

They lean in towards each other. They are about to kiss.
LUCY *breaks away.*

LUCY. That stuff's important, you know.

PETE *understands that this means a lot to* LUCY.

PETE. Aye. I know.

The moment has passed. They stand awkwardly.

LUCY. You ironed my pants.

PETE. Not just your pants.

LUCY. I wouldn't do that for anybody.

PETE. Aye, you would.

LUCY. No way.

PETE. If I asked you some day in the future. Maybe years from now. If I got down on one knee and said:

JACK. Dawn Donegal, I plight thee my troth.

PETE. Lucy Adamson, please will you wash and iron my underpants?

Knowing that I'd do it for you, that I have done it for you. If I asked you, you'd do it.

BEANIE. Are you asking?

LUCY. Or telling me?

JACK *and* PETE. Asking.

JACK. What's your answer?

BEANIE. Yes.

And what about LUCY? *Is she ready to open her heart to* PETE?

LUCY. Aye, mebbe.

BEANIE. I will if you will so will I.

JACK. Singing I will if you will so will I.

BEANIE. I will if you will.

JACK. I will if you will.

BEANIE *and* JACK. I will, if you will, so will I.

PETE *and* LUCY *lean in for that kiss but just before they do…Blackout.*

www.nickhernbooks.co.uk

facebook.com/nickhernbooks

twitter.com/nickhernbooks